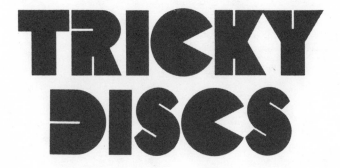

Ross R. Olney

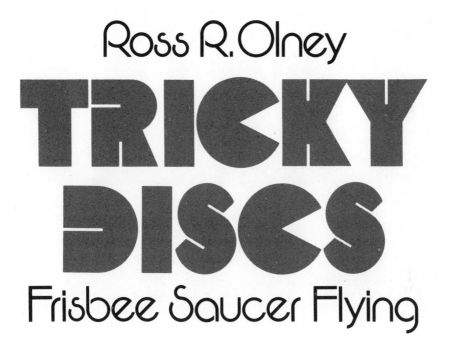

TRICKY DISCS

Frisbee Saucer Flying

Lothrop, Lee & Shepard Company
A Division of William Morrow & Co., Inc.
New York

By Ross R. Olney

How to Understand Soccer
The Young Runner
Drama on the Speedway
Roller Skating!! (with Chan Bush)
Tricky Discs: Frisbee Saucer Flying

J
796.2
O

TITLE-PAGE PHOTOGRAPH:
Mark Danna, an American disc flying champion, skims a disc right over the head of the photographer. (Ross R. Olney photo)

Library of Congress Cataloging in Publication Data
Olney, Ross Robert, (date)
  Tricky discs.
SUMMARY: Discusses the origin, care and transport of the Frisbee and other flying discs; techniques for trick throws and catches; games such as Guts, Ultimate, and Disc Golf.
1. Flying discs (Game)—Juvenile literature.   [1. Flying discs (Game)]   I. Title.
GV1097.F7046   796.2   78-31851
ISBN 0-688-41891-0   ISBN 0-688-51891-5 lib. bdg.

Frisbee® is a brand name and a registered trademark of Wham-O Mfg. Co.

Acknowledgments

The author would like to thank the following for photos, advice and technical information:

Alan Bonopane, International Frisbee disc Association
Jo Cahow, International Frisbee disc Association
Mike Conger, flying disc expert
Mark Danna, American flying disc champion
Mary Greenwood, Canadian flying disc champion
Darle L. Kerkenbush, Wham-O Manufacturing Company
Norm Kravitz, photographer and darkroom technician
Danny Mahr, Swedish flying disc champion
James E. Marvel, North Pacific Products Inc.
Goldy Norton, public relations
Deborah J. Olander, Parker Brothers
and especially Wayne Pinkstaff, a good friend who took time out from hockey, his first love, to help with photography on this book.

Contents

1

The Flying Disc

There are several theories on the origin of the exciting sport of flying disc flying. One is quite logical. The others demand a little more imagination.

But there is no question at all about why the sport has become so popular. You can barely go to a beach, a picnic, or an open field anymore without seeing discs whizzing about. Here's why.

You don't have to be big or strong or tall, or anything, to fly the disc. You can be a boy or a girl, a man or a woman. Little kids and grandparents fly discs. Just about everybody already does it, or can do it. And everyone can do it *well*, with just a little practice.

Champion disc flyers are not that much ahead of amateurs who toss discs at local parks.

It is a fresh, new sport where you get as much pure fun from the catch as from the throw.

Just feel a good flying disc. The smooth plastic is warm and appealing. The shape is attractive. The disc

Throwing the flying disc can be a pleasant, relaxing recreation.
(Ross R. Olney photo)

seems to want to spin away from you and float on the wind. It *wants* to play with you.

The venerable Smithsonian Institution recently recognized the flying disc with a comprehensive exhibition that included photos, demonstrations, and antique and modern discs. The National Air and Space Museum has a gallery devoted to flight for amusement, and the flying discs are on display.

Football, basketball, baseball, golf, and many other fun sports are expensive. With flying disc flying, all you need is a disc. Some people call them Frisbee discs, like those made by the Wham-O Company. Others call them Whiz Rings or Nerf discs or something else, and it doesn't make much difference which brand you buy—they are all inexpensive.

10

Flying the disc requires individual effort, but it doesn't have to be competitive. Disc flying can be a pleasant and relaxing activity in a harshly competitive world.

Flying the disc requires smoothness and polish, not muscles and force.

Dr. Stancil E. D. Johnson might have expressed it best of all. Johnson is a disc historian and a member of a championship team. He is also the author of the comprehensive book *Frisbee: A Practitioner's Manual.*

Johnson said, "When a ball dreams, it dreams it's a Frisbee."

Where did this toy for everybody come from? It is really nothing more than a carefully shaped plastic disc. There are many different models and styles from many different manufacturers, some of which fly better than others. Flying the disc has grown to a full-fledged national and international sport. They are even now speaking of making it an event in future Olympic Games.

Or it can be a wild and exciting competition.   (Ross R. Olney photo)

People have developed many different ways to play with the flying disc. This photograph shows tipping and spinning.   (Wayne Pinkstaff photo)

But where *did* it come from? You pick the story you like best.

Pheidippides was a Greek who became most famous as a runner. He was the one who determined the distance for a modern marathon. He was sent on a long run by his commander, Miltiades, to warn Athens of the approach of the Persian enemy.

What has only been hinted at until now is that young Pheidippides really dreamed of being a discus thrower.

True, he was a fine runner, and runners were high on the athletic ladder in ancient Greece. But the throwers of the discus were highest of all. The discus throw was the most popular event in the Grecian athletic games. The winning discus thrower was heralded as the greatest athlete.

Knowing that he was about to be sent on the most grueling run of his life, Pheidippides nervously waited outside the tent of Miltiades. At his side was his ever present discus, for he was always practicing his throw. But while he waited, Pheidippides began to fidget about, rubbing the discus on the ground. He did not know there was a hard rock just under the surface and the rock began to grind into the underside of the discus. Soon it was beginning to be hollowed out.

"Pheidippides!" snapped Miltiades. "I want you to get this message to Athens as quickly as possible!" The general thrust the scroll into Pheidippides' hand.

Turning toward Athens, Pheidippides squared his shoulders. With one last fond look at his discus, knowing he could not carry it along, he gave it a mighty throw. The discus (with the bottom accidentally hollowed somewhat) sailed far, far away from the amazed young runner.

"How did you *do* that?" Miltiades is reported to have asked, momentarily forgetting the important mission.

Of course, Pheidippides didn't know. In fact, he was already on his way toward Athens without a backward glance. And everybody knows that at the end of his journey, he dropped dead. A common Greek soldier picked up the discus of Pheidippides (it is *not* true that his name

Dogs play with the flying disc, too.
(Ross R. Olney photo)

was Frisbus) and so the very first flying disc of all was saved for future generations.

That story is possibly true. You decide.

In any case, there are those who give the ancient Greeks credit with or without Pheidippides. The famous statue of Discobolus, the discus thrower, is said by them to really be a Frisbee disc champion attempting a tricky overhand wrist flip.

Some people believe the flying disc did not appear until much later. They believe the disc was invented during the filming of the classic motion picture *I Am a Fugitive from a Chain Gang* (1932). Everybody from Hollywood believes this even if the rest of the United States doubts.

The story is that cameraman Antonio "Lens" Cinemataggio, an assistant to the third assistant in the second unit of the company, made a mistake and opened the

14

wrong can of film. The film he opened had already been shot. It was supposed to be on its way to the processing lab. Lens meant to open a new can to hand up to the assistant who did the camera loading.

Realizing his mistake, a mistake that cost the company forty-seven dollars since they had to reshoot that entire day's action, Lens was aghast. He knew his job hung in the balance. He had exposed the film to light and ruined it.

"Oh, darn!" he exclaimed. Then he grabbed the lid of the film can and threw it with all his might. It glided far out across the steamy swamp the company was using as a set and the story is that it barely missed actor Paul Muni before it landed.

So, perhaps, was born the flying disc.

The trouble is, in other parts of the country other stories have been accepted. In the Midwest they believe no history of the flying Frisbee disc that doesn't include sailing coffee can lids out over the wheat fields. Down South they feel that flying discs grew from the clay pigeons shooters use as targets. There is a rather foolish story circulating about how Paul Bunyan, the giant woodsman, used manhole covers as the original Frisbee discs, but you can accept that or not.

Paint can lids have been sailed and claims have been made that they were the original flying disc. Pie pans make fine flyers and at last we come to perhaps the most logical story of the creation of the Frisbee disc.

In Bridgeport, Connecticut, there was a bakery called

the Frisbie Pie Company or Frisbie Baking Company, according to which historian you believe. Though there is some controversy about whether the original flying disc was a pie plate or a cookie tin lid, it is well known that Frisbie's pies (and cookies too) had wide distribution up and down the eastern seaboard and were popular with the students at Yale University in neighboring New Haven.

Just why the first Yale student happened to throw the first pie plate (or cookie tin lid, if that is the case) has been lost in history. But at Middlebury College in Vermont there is a contending claim that the game of Frisbie was invented by five of their students in 1939.

That spring, the Delta Upsilon fraternity met to choose the delegate who would represent them at the national convention in Lincoln, Nebraska, in September. Five names were on the ballot, and the five were asked to leave the room while the vote was held.

Waiting outside, Richard Barclay (who turned out to be the one selected) suggested that they all go, sharing the expense money of the elected delegate. He was pretty sure he could borrow his aunt's Model A touring car, and they could sleep in the car or out in the open fields.

Come September, that is what they did. The Model A held up pretty well until somewhere in the Midwest, where they had a flat tire. As Elbert "Mole" Cole, Jr., tells it, he and Robert "Hawg" Gale didn't want to change the tire, so he started running slalom through the cornfield with Gale, who was captain of the ski team. And there, among the cornstalks, was a Frisbie pie pan, just lying there waiting to make history. Gale picked it up, spun it to Cole, and at the same time yelled, "Frisbie!"

Basketball player Paul "Togo" Eriksson joined the game while Barclay and Porter "Pete" Evans were changing the tire. All athletes, they quickly discovered the possibilities in flying the Frisbie tin, and by the time they got back to Middlebury, says Eriksson, they were experts.

From the DU fraternity house lawn, the game spread to the rest of the campus. The air was filled with flying pie pans and that spring, according to Cole, the whole student body almost flunked out.

Paul Eriksson thinks that the new sport was spread to other campuses by the fraternities and by debating teams. Certainly it caught on—you couldn't buy a pie tin in Middlebury, and when the new fad hit the other eastern campuses, the Frisbie company found that 5,000 of its pie pans were unreturned.

It is true that the Frisbie pie tin (or any pie tin, for that matter) does fly well. Not as well as the modern flying disc, of course, but well enough for Yale students to arrange games for distance and accuracy. This could also be the period when Lens Cinemataggio skimmed his film can lid. Perhaps this is when others began to fly coffee can lids, clay pigeons, and paint can covers, too.

Still, the flying of discs was pretty much confined to college campuses until the mid-1940s, when plastic was invented and a man by the name of Walter Frederick "Fred" Morrison came along. Morrison, the son of the man who invented sealed beam headlights, didn't wait for the invention of plastic.

He had a very inventive mind himself, and he was interested in the furor caused by the so-called "flying saucers" that might be invading the earth. Everybody was watching for them and a few people during that time even claimed to have seen one or more. Morrison, who had himself skimmed lids and plates, decided to try to improve the stability of the pie pan by adding a steel ring around its rim.

Most people believe the original flying disc was this Frisbie Pie Company pie plate. (International Frisbee disc Association photo)

The ring helped and the pie plate flew farther and smoother than ever before. But Morrison felt that something else was needed. Along came plastic and Morrison knew he had found the answer. He carved a disc of smooth plastic and it flew just *fine*.

It didn't land too well, though. Made of a butyl stearate blend, it tended to work well if the sun was up. But the minute the disc cooled down and landed on a hard surface, it would shatter into a million pieces.

These problems couldn't stop a man like Morrison. He would improve his blend and carve another disc. Finally he obtained an injection mold machine and began to pump out "saucers" by the hundreds. His selling method was unique. He would take a batch of saucers to the county fair in Pomona, California, where he had a booth. Once there, he would laboriously install an "invisible wire" as potential customers watched in wonder.

"Make some room for the wire," Morrison would shout as he "unreeled" and "attached" *nothing at all*.

Then he would demonstrate his saucer by appearing to hook it to the "wire." Finally he would toss it in a long, straight flight. The saucer did appear to be sliding along a wire.

As the people would push up to the booth to buy the saucer, Morrison would chuckle and say, "Well, the saucer is free . . . but the 'wire' is a penny a foot and comes in hundred-foot lengths."

The flight of Morrison's saucer was not nearly as good as today's flights, but it was good enough to make a tidy

Flying discs fly much like the wing of an airplane. Experts like this can keep a disc flying by airbrushing it. (Ross R. Olney photo)

profit for its inventor. More years drifted by and more than a few people in California had Morrison Flying Saucers. Morrison would hawk his wares on city streets and in parks and anywhere else a crowd gathered. Late in 1955, he was on a downtown street corner in Los Angeles when who should happen by but Rich Knerr and A. K. "Spud" Melin.

Knerr and Melin were the young men in charge of Wham-O, a marketing company in San Gabriel, California. Wham-O didn't make things for sale; rather, they arranged for things to be made and then marketed them. They were currently marketing a slingshot.

Things had been up and down at Wham-O, for it was a company that depended on fads for survival. Fads are hard to predict. But both Knerr and Melin saw a spark in the strange flying saucer of Fred Morrison. They saw something that could become popular.

So they bought Morrison's rights to the saucer and the

mold he had been using to make them. Soon, under the imprint of Wham-O, the plastic saucers came flying. The production line started on January 3, 1957, and it hasn't stopped since. More than one hundred million have flown out, in sixteen different models from this company alone.

But not all that many flew out at first. The saucers didn't catch on. Wham-O was sure they had a hit on their hands and they kept trying. They sent batches of the saucers to different parts of the country. These were real flying saucers. They had portholes and were made to look like Unidentified Flying Objects. They are worth quite a bit to collectors today.

What about the Frisbie Pie Company? Knerr was making a visit to the Ivy League colleges and heard the term "Frisbie." Now Harvard students were tossing pie tins and other flat objects around and they were calling "Frisbie!" the way a golfer would call "Fore!" Knerr liked the sound of the word, but not knowing of the pie company, he spelled it differently.

The world was introduced to the Frisbee® disc.

Still the boom didn't start. For Wham-O had in the meantime introduced another fad toy and it was sweeping the country. While thousands of Frisbee discs lay on the shelves, people all over the country were buying Hula Hoops.

They are still popular, but the day of the flying disc was coming. Ed Headrick, general manager and vice president of Wham-O, saw the Frisbee disc as more than a toy for casual tossing. He envisioned flying the disc as a

"Guts" is a game with the flying disc that takes nerve and lightning-fast reflexes. (Ross R. Olney photo)

serious competitive sport. So he developed and introduced the Professional Model Frisbee disc in 1964 and the Frisbee disc was on its way.

Other companies followed with their own type of flying disc. Some were made of soft foam plastic, some had holes in the middle, and some even had handles. They made discs that lit up in the night, some of them with tiny light bulbs and some with glowing chemicals.

Headrick also formed the International Frisbee Association, now known as the International Frisbee disc Association. The club has more than 85,000 members and continues to grow.

The game of Guts was invented in 1968 and in 1969

22

came the game of Ultimate. Both are now popular inter-scholastic and intercollegiate games.

Even the United States Navy became involved. The Navy decided that the flying disc flew so well that perhaps they could invent an airplane-dropped, disc-shaped battle-field flare in that shape. An involved secret study was launched, but that was the only thing launched. The plan failed.

Flying Disc World was first published in the 1970s. By then, 100-yard throws had become standard in rugged competitions. World Frisbee Championships were held in the Rose Bowl in Pasadena, California, in 1974. Champions from around the world competed before more than 55,000 spectators in the 1978 contest, for it is now an annual event.

By 1975, regional championship flying disc contests were being held around the country. The *International Frisbee Association Newsletter* was combined with *Flying Disc World* to become today's *Frisbee World,* a popular magazine with a wide circulation. The Smithsonian In-stitution sponsors a Frisbee disc Festival each September. In 1977 more than 5,000 people showed up to throw discs around.

Today, the flying of plastic discs is regarded as a serious competitive sport by thousands of enthusiasts. More thou-sands—hundreds of thousands—of fans regard the flying of discs as an enjoyable hobby and a relaxing pastime.

However you look at it, flying the disc is here to stay.

2
How the Disc Can Fly

There are dozens and dozens of different types of flying discs. There are Whiz Rings, Flingers, Saucer Tossers and, of course, the all-time favorite Frisbee disc.

Some of them are soft, some hard; some have holes in the center and some have lights for night flying. The book *Frisbee: A Practitioner's Manual,* lists more than seventy different flying discs in nine different categories such as antiques, toys, serious flyers, experimentals, and foreign-made discs.

Flying disc collecting has become a popular hobby. Some collectors who have been at it awhile have hundreds of discs, all different. Flying discs are traded, bought, sold, and advertised in club publications. Some are quite rare and are valuable to collectors. If you can find an original Frisbie Pie Company tin, a Morrison saucer, or any one of several other rare flying discs, you are in a fine bargaining position. Most collectors would give several of whatever they have for one of your treasures.

There are three different types of flying discs. There is the soft, spongy plastic "Nerf" type that has evolved into

Flying discs come soft and spongy, such as this one on the right.
(Parker Brothers photo)

They also come in a ring shape, with a hole in the center, like this one (left).
(North Pacific Products, Inc. photo)

They even come in different sizes, like this mini-disc (below).
(Ross R. Olney photo)

a whole series of Parker Brothers toys. They now have Nerf Rockets, Nerfman, Space Raider, and Nerf Gliders. These toys can be used in the home with little worry about damage to vases and windows, but they are not for the serious disc flyer. Recently, in fact, Parker has stopped production on the true Nerf disc in favor of the varieties mentioned above. The Nerf disc could become a collector's item.

Serious and competitive disc flyers will be more interested in the other two types of flying disc. The "halo" type of disc with the hole in the middle is most strongly represented by the "Whiz Ring" of North Pacific Products. There is a Mini Whiz Ring, a Regular Whiz Ring, and the Master Whiz Ring. The Mini is only 6½ inches wide, the Regular is 9¾ inches, and the Master 10⅜ inches wide.

More than just a plastic ring, the halo disc is an open airfoil that develops lift to fly. It has the advantage of being lighter in weight (this can also be a disadvantage in certain windy conditions) and easier to catch. The ring type of disc is an especially good model for younger children. They can throw it and catch it more quickly and with less training.

Solid research and development produced the excellent flying characteristics of the ring discs. A correctly thrown ring will have neutral flight characteristics. It will fly true and straight without sagging to the right or the left. Of course if the ring is tilted as it is released, it will curve in that direction.

Manufacturers of the ring type of disc claim that the strong wrist "snap" necessary to fly the third, closed type of disc is not necessary with the ring. This is true to the extent that the ring won't fly as far as the closed disc with the same soft toss, but it will fly straight and under control.

A three-year-old can get good flights from a ring and adults can have fun with them. They are easy and accurate. These discs are just right for certain games like Ringer and Accuracy Toss (see Chapter 6).

The most popular flying disc type is the closed disc, the Frisbee disc type. Many manufacturers make this type of disc, but the Frisbee disc has long been the most popular. There are probably more Frisbee discs than all the other discs combined.

Frisbee discs from Wham-O come in several different models and sizes, including a new Player's Handbook model that comes with detailed instructions on how to fly it. Frisbee discs also come in Regular, an economy model for beginners, Super Pro, Professional, All American, and Master models. On some the flight characteristics are slightly different, and on others the colors are different. There is also a Frisbee Moonlighter that glows in the dark for night flights.

Many experts feel that the Frisbee Pro is the best all-around flying disc available today. Advertised for the "advanced" player, the Pro offers distance and stability to every player irrespective of skill.

What makes a disc fly? The same thing that makes a

coffee can lid or a pie pan fly. A disc, any disc, is one form of an airfoil. A flat disc will fly. If a giant such as Paul Bunyan could actually throw a manhole cover with a flat, spinning action, it would fly.

The difference between a pie pan and a manhole cover, other than weight of course, is that the pan has form. It is bulged in the middle and creates a truer airfoil, so it flies better.

Scientifically speaking, there must be a lifting force to counteract gravity. This lift is present with a flying disc because of the curved edge that is always leading when in flight.

As the wind hits the front of a disc, it splits over and under. But as it goes over it is forced up because of the curved front, just like an airplane wing. This creates a low pressure area directly above the disc's center surface. Air from underneath moves up to fill this low pressure area, carrying the disc with it, and the disc rises.

Further, when the disc is tipped slightly upward it has, according to pilots, a "positive angle of attack." You can get this same feeling by holding your hand out the window of the car as it is moving (making sure first that nothing will hit it). Hold it flat, edge to the wind. As you then tilt your hand up or down, you can feel the very strong forces acting against it.

There is even more to the marvel of a flying disc than this.

1. The *spin* of the disc provides stability. You can test this very easily by just tossing a flying disc. Don't throw

Canadian champion Mary Greenwood keeps a disc in the air by tipping it with one finger. (Ross R. Olney photo)

it correctly, with a spin. Just pitch it out there. It doesn't fly well at all, does it? But if you throw it correctly, with a spin, it has stability. It continues spinning on the same plane, like a gyroscope.

2. The *forward motion* of a flying disc provides the lift to keep it in the air. It is the forward motion, imparted

29

TRICKY DISCS

by your throw, which causes the low pressure area above
and the higher pressure area below that lift the disc.

The harder the throw, the faster the disc will go through

*Another fancy way to keep a disc flying is by tipping it from under your
legs.* (Wayne Pinkstaff photo)

This expert can bounce the disc back and forth between the backs of his hands. (Wayne Pinkstaff photo)

the air and the greater the lift will be. And the greater the lift, the longer the flight.

3. The *position* or *attitude* of the disc as it leaves your hand will control the path the disc takes through the air.

(a) *Pitch.* If the leading edge of the disc is tilted up, the disc will rise. If it is tilted up high enough and the disc has been thrown into the wind, it will return almost

31

It is possible to fly the disc between your legs by tipping from one hand to another, as this expert is doing. (Ross R. Olney photo)

directly to your hand. If the leading edge is tilted up but the disc is thrown down, it will bounce on a cushion of air (this takes practice) and then rise on away from you. Of course if you tilt the leading edge of the disc down as you throw it, it will hit the ground.

(b) *Roll.* The disc can be released with the right or left side higher. If the right side is higher at the instant of release from your hand, the disc will curve away to the left. If the left side is higher, it will curve away to the right.

All of these factors must, with a flying disc, be imparted by the thrower as the disc is released. It cannot accelerate or change its initial force or attitude. It can only decelerate.

One other factor is involved in the flight of the flying disc. The *force* of the flight is the power you have put into it at the moment of release. But you'll learn as you read on in this book that force does not always mean muscle. It can also mean skillful technique in throwing.

So the disc, whether it is solid or has a hole in it, passes through the air almost exactly like the wing of an airplane. It has aerodynamic lift. The only difference is that a disc must spin to keep its stability. Otherwise it would just flop to the ground.

Beginning disc flyers sometimes have difficulty getting enough spin (by getting a strong enough wrist action), and the disc tends to wobble. The more you cock your wrist, the more you snap it, the more spin you will achieve. Thus, the more stable the flight will be.

Don't let anybody trick you at the next flying disc gathering by getting you to go look for a "left-handed" disc. Flying discs spin equally well clockwise or counterclockwise. In fact, the same disc from the same right-handed thrower will fly clockwise from one type of throw and counterclockwise from another. Just the reverse is true if the thrower is left-handed.

Assuming a right-handed thrower, these basic throws (see next chapter) will spin clockwise:

Backhand

Underhand

TRICKY DISCS

These basic throws will spin counterclockwise from a right-handed thrower:

Overhand Wrist Flip

Thumber

Sidearm

Reverse the above lists of throws if you are a left-handed thrower, for the disc will spin just the opposite.

One of the best times to throw the flying disc is when there is no wind at all. The trouble is, weather doesn't always cooperate with our desire to have fun throwing. So you must adjust your throw to compensate for wind speed and direction. You must do this before you throw, imparting everything into the throw you have calculated. After the disc leaves your hand, it is too late.

This presents yet another consideration when throwing, for the *angle of release* must be accounted for. On any flight the disc is released with a much greater angle, side to side, than you might at first think. This angle can be nearly vertical if the wind speed is high or the direction wrong. The angle of release can be seen in many of the photos in this book. For now, remember that a disc is almost never released exactly flat, or horizontal. Remember, this is the side-to-side angle, not the front-to back angle.

The spin of a disc tends to carry it off to the side. If a clockwise spinning disc is released level, it will fall off to the right in the direction of its spin. So it is tilted to its left about 45 degrees as it is released. Because of the spin, the left edge will rise early in the flight and the disc will soon be flying level.

Don't worry too much about these techniques if you are just starting your career of disc flying. These skills seem to come naturally with practice.

Do practice. Some kinds of practice aren't much fun, but it is fun to throw the disc. Improvement in your skill and technique will come quickly.

Following the suggestions in the next few chapters, try it your own way. Nothing is locked in. Disc flying is still new and improving every day. Exciting new throws are being developed by young flyers. Throws once thought

Some experts can keep a disc flying between them while whirling around and around, as these two are doing. (Wayne Pinkstaff photo)

But finally the disc must come to a stop, though not often in such a fancy way. (Wayne Pinkstaff photo)

to be impossible are now being accomplished regularly, and longer distances are being reached.

If you decide to become a contestant in competitions, you will see other competitors trying new and zany throws and wild new catches. Try them yourself. Work on them. Unlike the difference between a pro tennis player and a Sunday afternoon player, the distance between a pro disc thrower and a beginner is small.

Thousands and thousands of new disc flyers are in the sport for the pure fun of it. They know the Frisbee disc flies long and straight and true, but they don't worry about how it does it. They just enjoy it.

3

Basic Disc Throws

The best way to start having fun flying the disc is with the favorite throw of disc fans. This throw might not be the best one for tough, competitive games like Guts (Chapter 6) but for fun flying, the Backhand is still the one.

As you read these instructions, follow the illustrations. Then do it yourself, for that is the best way of all to learn the fun, accuracy and speed of the disc. Always remember, it should be *fun*.

The Backhand

Relax, take a deep breath, loosen your body, bend and flex your knees slightly. Once you learn this throw, you have learned the most basic of all the basic throws. There are others, as you will see, but this is the place to begin.

Take the disc in your off hand and place it in your throwing hand. Press down on the top with your thumb and press your index finger along the rim. Allow your other three fingers to press up on the bottom, with the last two fingers (the fourth and little finger) slightly curled under the rim, in the cheek. The thumb will be pressing down very near where the middle finger is pressing up and will be about an inch and a half from the end of the index finger along the rim.

Get used to this positioning of the hand on the disc. But wait a minute. Suppose your three underside fingers feel more natural straight rather than bent back toward the cheek? Then do it that way. Be natural above everything else. Be comfortable. The basic grips must feel right to you. Don't worry that much about what the thrower next to you is doing.

The backhand, shown here by Swedish Champion Danny Mahr, is the most basic of all the disc throws. (Ross R. Olney photo)

Hold the disc until you feel comfortable with the grip. It is very important in these beginning steps that you don't strain or attempt to force your fingers, hands, or body into unnatural positions. Also at this point, it is important to resist the "lady finger grip." This is a grip with limp fingers, holding the disc by the fingertips. *Grasp* the disc. Hold it firmly as you master the basic Backhand.

Exactly how hard do you hold a disc? Somebody once explained that you hold a disc the same way you hold a canary. "Grip it like a small bird," they said. "Tight enough to keep it from flying away, but loose enough so that you won't kill it."

Don't worry about it. It will come to you if you practice.

To prepare for the Backhand throw, stand with your feet a couple of feet apart and in line with each other. Your body will be facing away from the target at a 90-degree angle. You will be at right angles to the target. If you are right-handed, your right side will be toward the target. If you are left-handed, your left side will be toward the target. Study the illustrations.

At this point your weight will be more on your back foot (away from the target) and will shift even more as you cock your arm and wrist to throw. But as the arm is brought forward and the wrist is snapped, the weight will naturally shift to the forward foot.

The angle of release should not be flat, or horizontal, though many disc throwers advise it. You will get better distance and more accuracy if the disc is tilted down at the outside edge. The disc will turn in the direction of its spin, so if it is tilted at release it will flatten out during its flight. Start out with an angle of about 45 degrees; then, as you gain skill (and as wind conditions vary), this can be adjusted.

Try to make your actual throw nearer waist high than up around your chest. This will help in endurance later on, when you might want to throw for hours.

Let's get ready. Unlock your elbow and keep your arm relaxed. The wrist action you impart will be the key to your throw. You cannot just throw a flying disc with your arm and hand and expect a good flight. Cock your wrist back away from the target as you prepare to throw. Do not tuck the disc into your body (your elbow should not point at the target).

With your wrist cocked, bring the disc back across your body until it is about even with your off-arm. For best results, pick a target about 20 yards away for these first exercises.

Bring the swing forward with your arm and elbow, keeping the elbow in as close to the body as feels comfortable. As the wrist moves past the elbow, snap it forward and release the disc. This should be about a foot or so past your body. Follow through so that your hand is pointing at the target. As you do this, remember the angle of release.

If the disc goes too much to the left (assuming a right-handed thrower), you have released it too soon. If it goes too far to the right of the target, you have held it too long. A few throws will quickly correct such mistakes.

A behind-the-back throw is not difficult, especially as done here by Canadian Champion Mary Greenwood. (Ross R. Olney photo)

You want the disc to fly smoothly, level and straight to the target, with as little wobble as you can manage.

According to expert disc flyers, one of the most common mistakes of a beginner is to rotate the wrist. Your palm should not face up as you release no matter what you see other beginners doing. Nor should you lunge forward as you throw, bringing your rear foot up off the ground. Most of the power from the throw will come from your wrist if you are doing it right. The rear foot might rise slightly, but the toes should still be in contact with the ground.

Watch the target, not the disc. If you are turning too far as you wind up, your head will tend to turn away from the target.

TRICKY DISCS

The whole action should be smooth and comfortable. It should feel natural. The action of throwing a disc is storing up energy with the wind-up and releasing it with the throw.

With concentration and practice, this will soon be a natural action and the disc will fly straight to the target. By tilting the disc slightly in the direction you want it to go just as you release it, you can get it to curve. Try it. Practice until you can get it to curve out and in to the target every time.

You will see players in contests running up to the line before releasing the disc. Some even turn one full turn to help build momentum. Fine. Try it if you wish. But first of all master the basic Backhand, then go to the fancier approaches.

The Sidearm

This is another basic throw you'll see wherever disc fans gather. The preferred grip for this throw is the two-finger grip. This is a somewhat more difficult grip for a more difficult throw, but you can learn it with practice.

Grasp the disc in the groove of your hand between the thumb and forefinger. The thumb should press down on the top of the disc directly over the forefinger, which is pressing up. Place the middle finger into the cheek under the rim of the disc. The other two fingers are not used, and can be curled into the palm.

Note that the disc will be spinning counterclockwise

Greenwood has just thrown the disc from between her legs.

(Ross R. Olney photo)

when you release it from a Sidearm throw (if you are right-handed, the opposite is true if you are a lefty). Don't get locked in too tightly on the finger positions, though. If it feels better to you to curl your forefinger into the cheek and then not use the other three fingers, do it that way. Practice both ways, then choose.

With this Sidearm throw you will be standing with your *left* side facing the target. Keep your feet wide apart

43

and with the weight on the rear foot. The weight should shift to the front foot as you throw. You might feel a little discomfort in your hand at first, but relax and try the throw anyhow.

Hold the disc to your right a little higher than with the Backhand, but not chest high. Cock the wrist and keep the palm up with the disc tilted slightly so that the leading edge is down. The palm should remain face up during and after the throw, with no wrist rotation.

Now bring the disc up in an arch so that it is up behind you. The throwing motion should be in a downward arch and straight out, with the weight shifting as you bring your arm forward. During the throw, the elbow should remain in close to the body. The wrist will trail behind the elbow but just as it moves forward of the elbow, snap it. The disc should roll off the middle finger just as you release it.

Go ahead and throw it, imparting the spin with an uncocking of the wrist as you release. Do it with a snap. You'll note that there is less arm motion with this throw than with the Backhand.

The more you cock your wrist back, the more power you will have at the moment of the throw. Practice this throw until it feels right to you, until the disc sails away in a straight line, leveling itself and heading straight for the target without falling off right or left. Resist the temptation to rotate your wrist. The palm should be facing up.

The Underhand

Still another basic throw you should master before going on to the trick throws is the Underhand. The disc is thrown with a bowling action with this one, but the grip is the same as that used for the Backhand.

So place your fingers with the forefinger along the rim, your thumb on top and the other three fingers underneath. This time, though, you will be standing directly facing the target. Distribute your weight equally on both feet, with your feet comfortably apart.

Shift your weight slightly to the right foot (if you are right-handed; opposite if you are left-handed), then rotate the hips to the right. Bring your throwing arm back behind you as though you were getting ready to release a bowling ball.

Step forward so that the weight is shifting to your left foot and bring your throwing arm forward at the same time. When your arm is directly out in front of you, un-cock your wrist and release the disc.

It will help if you don't put too much power into this throw the first few times. Allow your arm and wrist to do the work, though experts (and, eventually, you) will get a good deal of power from the untwisting of the hips from right to left (or left to right with a southpaw). Practice until you get a smooth, wobble-free flight to a short-range target, then attempt to increase the distance gradually.

Danny Mahr of Sweden lines up for a thumber. (Ross R. Olney photo)

The Thumb Throw

This is a high speed throw, but still a basic disc maneuver. Later you will read about the game of Guts. The Thumb Throw is one of the main weapons in this contest because a "thumber" has a tendency to sink quickly as it dies. The disc is very difficult to catch. Still, the Thumb Throw is not a difficult throw to master.

A Thumb Throw will spin counterclockwise from a right-hander, clockwise from a left-hander. The fastest disc throw ever clocked by the International Frisbee disc

Association was a Thumb Throw. It traveled 105 miles per hour!

Jam your thumb into the underside cheek of the disc as shown in the illustration. Let your other four fingers grip the disc on top. A right-handed thrower should have the left side facing the target. The feet should be in a natural stance with the weight somewhat more on the right foot as you lean back to prepare for the throw. Cock your wrist as you bring the disc back into your upper arm.

With the wrist cocked, bring the arm down in a sweeping motion, leading with the elbow. Sweep down between the shoulder and the hip and as you do so, shift the weight forward more to your left foot. You'll be pivoting on your right foot at the same time.

The elbow should stay in close to the body, and as the arm moves keep the palm up. As the disc is brought past your hip, uncock your wrist and release it at about a 45-degree angle. With practice you'll be able to snap the thumb at the instant of release, giving the disc another boost of power on its way to the target.

If the disc turns over in flight, you are falling into the habit of rotating your wrist during the throw. Practice and you'll get the hang of this one. It isn't difficult.

If you want the disc to rise after a Thumb Throw, tilt the leading edge upward slightly as it is released. If you want it to drop, the disc face should be nearly vertical, then throw *hard*. A downward-dropping, sideways-moving, counterclockwise-spinning disc is very difficult to catch. That's why they use this throw in Guts games. A

47

An overhand wrist fling is fired at Canadian Champion Mary Greenwood, in the foreground. (Ross R. Olney photo)

Thumb Throw is not, however, the most accurate throw, so use it with care.

The Overhand Wrist Fling

The experts who admire this throw consider it to be one of the most beautiful throws of all.

Using a grip similar to the Thumb Throw, place the disc into the wedge of your hand with all four fingers on top and your thumb underneath. The thumb should be squeezing against your middle finger. If you want to try a slightly different Overhand Wrist Fling grip to see which

48

one you like better, you might also throw a few with your forefinger along the outer rim and only three fingers on top. The thumb will still be securing the disc against the middle finger.

In either case, the fingers should be spread out for better stability and the thumb should be in a comfortable position. If that means moving the thumb closer to the rim or farther from it, do so.

If you are right-handed, your left side should be facing the target. The feet should be in line and in a normal, comfortable stance as for the other basic throws. Your weight should shift from your back (right) leg to the left leg as the throw progresses.

The counterclockwise spin will tilt the disc to the left during its flight, so you will want to tilt the right edge down at release to compensate.

Lock your throwing arm straight and bring the disc behind you as shown in the illustration. Cock the wrist and shift the weight as described. The disc can be up and over the hand so far that it almost rests on the lower forearm.

The power of the Overhand Wrist Fling comes from the wrist and from the uncoiling of the body as the throw is generated. With the elbow locked, bring the arm out almost parallel to the ground. Keep the wrist cocked as your weight shifts forward to the left foot and the hips begin to uncoil to the left.

As you reach the release point in front of you, quickly uncock the wrist, snapping it forward as you release.

Danny Mahr shows proper form leading up to over-hand wrist fling.
(Ross R. Olney photo)

Then he lets go!
(Ross R. Olney photo)

Your hand should be pointing at the target, palm down, and your hips should continue their follow through to the left. Try to remember not to twist the wrist. It should cock back to the right, then snap to the left. It should not rotate or turn sideways.

In competitions, some experts add a complete body turn (or more) to the lead-in to this throw in order to build up stored power. Like the discus throwers of old Greece, they spin up to the throwing line and release with a tremendous surge of power (often accompanied by a loud grunt from the strain).

The Hooked Thumb Throw

If all goes well, this one should start out upside down and finish right side up. Since the game of Guts requires players to catch the disc, this is another throw that can be difficult and confusing during that type of competition.

It is the final basic disc throw and should be added to your group of throws. Once you have these six mastered (and some of the catches in the following chapter) *you* will be one of the experts in any group of disc flyers. Then, if you wish, you can go on to some of the trick throws in Chapter Five.

For the Hooked Thumb Throw, put the disc in the wedge of your throwing hand with the thumb on the cheek pinching against the joint of the forefinger on the rim. The other three fingers can be folded into the palm of the hand. Hold tightly between the thumb and the fore-finger joint.

Your left side should be facing the target if you are a right-hander, the opposite if you are a left-handed thrower. Swing the disc back and up behind your head with the bottom facing toward you. Feet should be in the same position as for the Thumb Throw. The throw will be the same as the Thumb Throw or the Sidearm Throw, with the elbow leading the arm across the body and close in.

Twist your hips to the right, then bring the disc down in an arc. The disc should be at about a 45-degree angle with the bottom up and the disc tilted away from you at the point of release. Twisting your hips to the left (for a right-handed thrower) will add force to the throw. This should be done just as the disc passes your left hip, at the point where you uncock your wrist to release.

Practice will help you get the disc to turn over during its flight. With this throw as with every other one, it will help if you follow through. Your hand should be pointing at the target after the disc has been released.

These six basic throws should be practiced over and over again until you have each one of them perfected. That is the fun of flying the disc. The whole point is to find some excuse to go out and throw and throw. You needn't be competitive about it. Take it easy. Learn the basic throws, master them but don't allow them to master you. Take them one at a time or all together.

If you need an excuse to go out throwing, now you have it.

4

Catching the Flying Disc

There is another great beauty to the sport of flying disc flying. It is just as much fun to catch a disc as it is to throw it.

Let's imagine you are a baseball pitcher out on the field practicing. You can either run after the ball every time you throw it (and that would be a drag), or you can get a pal to help you by catching.

You might have a fine time, but unless he or she has dreams of being a catcher on the team, your friend is probably going to be bored.

Not with the flying disc, though. Throwing it is fun and catching it is fun. Every time you catch it, you get to throw it back. So you and your friend are out there throwing and catching and both of you are enjoying it.

Here's a fact every disc flinger must face. *The idea is to catch the disc.* That should be the end result of a throw, in spite of all the talk about tricky or beautiful catches. The disc should not hit the ground. There are going to be times when catching seems impossible. You have set

Sometimes two players manage to catch the disc at the same time. (Wayne Pinkstaff photo)

Sometimes three *manage.*   (Ross R. Olney photo)

yourself up with a frantic scramble through bushes, bird watchers, other games, and spectators. The disc is floating down . . . floating down—but oh!, just beyond your reach.

You have misjudged.

So leap, twist, jump, catch it however you can. Grab it, trap it, clap it. A catch with no style is a thousand times better than no catch at all. Even the experts have salvage catches when all else fails.

Sure, you want to make a beautiful catch, but when the chips are down, catch it any way you can.

There is a school of thought that says the thumbs up position of the hand is best for disc catching. Another school says it should be thumbs down for disc catching. Each group argues that the nerves in the specific spot where the disc will hit (between the thumb and forefinger on the soft part of the hand) are best used by *their* choice of hand position.

Each says that the slight difference in impact against the nerves of the skin triggers the hand to close more efficiently. Neither school considers the set-up and preparation for the catch, or the fact that the hand should really be closing before the disc hits it. But that doesn't matter. Disc flyers enjoy getting together and debating such minute details.

Thumbs up or thumbs down? Try it this way. If the disc is coming in waist high or higher, catch it with the thumb down. If it is coming in at a height below the waist, catching it will probably be easier with the thumb up.

Either way, keep the hand relaxed and in a general C-shape. The fingers should be ready, but not rigid. You may knock a finger or even break a fingernail at first, but it will all come with practice.

Certainly, expert catchers begin their catch before the disc hits the hand. They begin their catch as the disc is leaving the hand of the thrower. They watch and calculate the type of throw to determine speed and spin. They consider wind direction and speed. As the flight progresses, they move to the spot where they think the disc will land. Throughout their move they are watching and recalculating as outside influences (a puff of extra wind, a tree branch, a kite string, etc.) alter the course of the disc.

Timing the flight of a disc can be baffling. A disc doesn't move through the air like a ball. It takes more than merely clawing the hand around it to catch it. A disc sometimes slides off; it floats, it parachutes down. Most experts recommend bringing the hand to the disc only at the moment of contact. They feel this will bring into play all the information you have picked up as you watch the flight. Then, at the last moment, bring your hand to the point of contact and close it. Beautiful!

If you want to listen to the experts, they will also suggest that you learn to catch with the hand you do not use to throw. This saves wear and tear on the hand. Do what feels best to you. You can always become a switch-catcher, learning to catch with either hand. Few throws will elude you when you have polished this skill.

What you will really have to learn is to *unlearn* how

Sometimes you just tip the disc to a nearby friend, not catching it at all.
(Ross R. Olney photo)

*If you are really tired, you can just catch the disc on the end of your finger
and nail-delay it for awhile.* (Ross R. Olney photo)

to catch a ball. Or at least put that skill in storage during your disc flying. The disc is spinning and will try to spin off your hand the moment it touches it. That's why it will be more difficult at first to catch a disc that is spinning counterclockwise. Such a spin will instantly tend to bounce away off the side of your hand. A clockwise spin will roll across your hand first, giving you a fraction of a second more time to close on it.

Here are some basic catches to practice on. Get them to the point where you seldom miss, then go on to the trick catches if you like.

The Sandwich Catch

This is a basic two-handed catch that is easy and still looks good. Just clap your hands together, one on top of the disc and one on the bottom. Trap the disc between

You can also nail-delay a disc even if it is upside down.
(Ross R. Olney photo)

58

You'll look like an expert if you make a trick catch like this behind-the-back catch.

your palms as it passes between them. Of course the top hand is palm down and the bottom hand palm up.

A variation of this is to catch the disc between your hands, only by the edges rather than top and bottom. With open hands about a foot apart, wait for the disc to approach. Then, at the right instant, close on it and grasp the edges.

Behind the Back

This one looks very tricky, but it isn't all that difficult. You will always draw a gasp from the onlookers with this catch, for they will quickly peg you as an expert. The thing that makes it a little more difficult than a simple Sandwich Catch is that you must make the catch blind. That is, at the moment you catch the disc, you don't see it. So planning ahead is very important.

Face the thrower and bend and flex your knees so that you can make small adjustments at the last minute as the disc approaches. It is best to try this one when the

59

The player cannot see the disc when the catch is made in this fancy behind-the-back catch.

(Ross R. Olney photo)

disc is coming waist high, though experts can leap and catch it or drop to their knees (or even bend over backward) to make the catch.

Don't reach behind you for the disc when the throw is made. Wait and watch, adjusting your position. You might have to make some quick moves very near the catching point and your arms will be needed for balance. If you are going to catch the disc with your right hand, turn 90 degrees to the right (so your left side is facing the target) just before the disc arrives. Left-handed, do just the opposite.

Bring your arm behind you waist high with the palm up and the hand in a C-shape. The flexed knees can quickly move you up or down a few inches in the final

60

moment. If you twist your left shoulder to the right (or opposite), you can follow the flight of the disc as long as possible before you lose sight of it behind your back.

This is all a matter of practice and timing. It appears more difficult than it really is. That is why it will draw admiration from spectators.

Between the Legs

This is easier than the Behind the Back because you can watch the disc all the way into your hand. This catch can be made with both feet on the ground, with one foot on the ground, and with both feet in the air. The last one might not be easier than the Behind the Back, though,

A delayed catch almost allows the disc to get by before you reach out and snag it.
(Ross R. Olney photo)

since it takes some agility as well as timing and judgment.

To make the catch with both feet on the ground, stand facing the thrower with the legs spread apart. An accurate thrower is a big help with this catch. Flex the knees. As the disc approaches, adjust your position as necessary. Then, when you have set yourself, reach from behind and between your legs with your palm up and make the catch.

You can try this same catch with still another variation. Make the catch *behind* you by reaching from front to back between your spread legs.

Face the thrower for the one-leg-in-the-air catch. As the disc arrives, adjust your position so that it will be lower than waist high; then, if you are a right-hander, turn your left side toward the disc. Raise your leg, reach under and make the catch.

The trick in making the catch with both feet off the ground is the timing of the jump. Everything else remains the same. You must position yourself correctly, but at the last instant leap into the air. Just reach through the legs and make the catch palm up.

You might not believe it, but a mistake of many beginners is jumping too high prior to this catch. More often than you might think, the disc will pass below the outstretched fingers of the catcher.

Behind the Head

Have you the confidence to try this one? Spectators will love you for it, especially if the disc comes very, very close

You can stall a catch by bouncing the disc off your elbow a few times.
(Ross R. Olney photo)

to your head as you catch it. This is another catch where an accurate throw is a great help. You want the disc to arrive about head high, but you will be positioned facing the thrower with knees flexed to make small adjustments.

As the disc arrives, turn so that your left side is toward it (for a right-hander). Keep your knees bent. When the disc is a few inches away, bend your head forward and make the catch with your palm-down hand just behind your head.

It is possible to leap for a disc coming in too high and still make a fine Behind the Head catch. It is also possible to do a deep knee bend and, squatting, make the catch. It is also possible to catch the disc in your hand after it has ricocheted (ouch!) off the back of your head.

It will smart, but the cheers from the people watching

Or bounce it off your fingers from under your leg.

(Ross R. Olney photo)

will soothe the pain. On the other hand, being too timid will often mean the disc will fly past your head just beyond the reach of your fingers. No cheers follow this common mistake.

The Finger Catch

This is an interesting catch when the disc is coming in about head high and floating. Once you get the hang of moving your finger in the direction of the spin of the disc, it is an easy catch. Meanwhile, there are some disc catchers who move their finger *against* the spin. Try each way and see what you can accomplish.

You will have better luck with this catch if you stand facing the thrower. Allow the disc to float almost past before you place your finger just inside the trailing edge. Then, as the disc settles, move your finger with the direction of the spin, slowing the spin more and more. Or, move your finger *against* the direction, slowing the spin much more rapidly.

The wrist should rotate as the hand and finger are moved with or against the spin. The disc will descend into your hand. Practice until you can just get your finger into contact with the disc as it is settling. Don't jab at the disc or it will only flop off and flutter to the ground.

Throughout these catches, keep in mind that it isn't always the smooth and perfect catch that distinguishes the expert. Disc flying is fairly new as a sport, in spite of its ancient history. New throws and catches are being tried all the time. Even the experts miss. Sometimes, in fact, they miss more than the casual player, for they are willing to try new, different, more difficult maneuvers.

So go ahead and try. Practice throwing and catching. Watch your positioning just prior to the catch (something that more accurately separates the expert from the amateur). Eventually you will have these catches down solidly and will be ready for the group in the next chapter.

5

Trick Throws and Catches

For pure distance or pure accuracy, you have learned the throws you need. For speed, too, and catching fun. Trick throws and trick catches, on the other hand, are for show. They *look* good.

Some of them look *very* good.

Here's a hint. Don't practice on these tricky moves to the extent that they alter the basic style you have worked to develop. Rather, use the style to work on the trick throws and catches. Just do them for what they are—fun.

Here are a few of them. With practice you'll develop some of your own fancy throws and catches.

The Finger Flip

You'll need timing and a good wrist snap, but otherwise this throw is easy. You can do it with any finger (the forefinger is probably best) or any pointed object. Whatever you do, don't go for distance at the beginning. Pick a spot a few yards out and try to get a smooth flight.

66

A knee tip with the disc upside down is a very tricky move, but this expert is handling it. (Wayne Pinkstaff photo)

Then, as you polish your technique, extend the target distance. A 20-yard throw is excellent.

There are two ways to manage this harmless little disc throw. Stand at a 45-degree angle to the target, your left side closer if you are right-handed. You will want to release the disc at about a 45-degree angle as well.

Using your left forefinger to hook and hold the disc, place the throwing finger of your right hand under the rim as shown in the illustration. Twist the disc slightly

These two freestyle experts are passing a spinning disc between them while accomplishing acrobatic moves. Very fancy. (Ross R. Olney photo)

away from the target, then with a quick, spinning motion, snap it forward and on its way. You'll quickly get the hang of this with a little practice.

A snappy and attractive way to throw is the Finger Flip combined with the Disc Spin. It is not difficult to get a disc spinning on the end of your finger by hooking the finger under the rim and then spinning it. You'll see that it almost stabilizes and that with a little practice you can keep the disc spinning as long as you wish.

For the throw, just spin the disc off your finger at the proper time. Control will come quickly. Give yourself a mental countdown so that your mind and hand will be in rhythm. As you are spinning, count down, ". . . five . . . four . . . three . . . two . . . one . . ." then, in that same rhythm, let it fly. At the instant of release, snap your wrist forward. You should then follow through with your palm up and your finger pointing at the target.

Behind-the-Back Backhand

The Backhand is one of the most accurate, easy throws of the disc. It is fairly easy to move from the regular Backhand to this throw, an exciting crowd-pleaser that will make you stand out on any field. It is much easier than it looks, yet it is still quite accurate and good for many yards of distance.

Here's how.

Stand as though you were going to throw a normal Backhand, with your right side toward the target if you

A very tricky squatting be-hind-the-back throw.

are a right-hander. Grip the disc in the normal Backhand grip—thumb on top, forefinger along the outside rim, and fingers underneath. Swing the disc out toward the target.

So far, everything you have done indicates a normal Backhand. But don't release the disc. Instead, begin a spiral motion of your throwing arm around and behind you. At the same time, begin to pivot on your left foot as you twist your hips back to the right. Begin to raise your left arm toward the target.

Your right arm will swing down near your right hip, and the disc will be turned vertical to pass. Continue to twist the hips and bring the arm around your back. Your hips and shoulders will line up with the target. With the body twisted completely around so that the left side is facing the target, and with the arm all the way around behind you, uncock your wrist and release the disc.

The arm will be in solid contact with the back as you follow through. You may even strike yourself in the back but it won't hurt. If it does, adjust your throw a little.

Meanwhile, the disc will already be on its way for an accurate flight.

This throw is all the more fun because it is deceptive. Nobody but you knows until the last instant whether you are going to throw a blistering Backhand or a much softer Behind-the-Back Backhand. Use this to add flavor and color to your disc flying.

Behind-the-Back Sidearm

This is another exciting variation that will still give you reasonable distance and accuracy. Start with the normal two-finger Sidearm grip with the disc in the groove or wedge of your hand, the thumb on top and the forefinger underneath. Curl the middle finger underneath into the cheek to give more stability to the throw.

With your left side (if you're a right-hander) toward the target, bring the disc up to above shoulder height as though you were going to throw a Sidearm. Keep your feet apart with your weight more on the rear foot. Cock your wrist and bend your knees slightly. Now bring your arm down and behind you. The disc will be almost vertical with your palm upward. The top of the disc will, of course, be toward you, the underneath side away, for this Sidearm-style throw.

Twist your hips and thrust your lower half forward a little so that you won't hit yourself with your hand or the disc. Bring your arm toward the target, thrust forward a little bit more, uncock your wrist and release the disc.

A difficult two-handed catch by two disc flying freestyle experts.
(Ross R. Olney photo)

It should just barely clear your rear end and be tilted back to about a 45-degree angle as it is released. The top edge of the disc is away from your body, the bottom toward you.

Under-the-Leg Sidearm

Here's another fancy throw that is fun to execute and crowd-pleasing if you have an audience. Of the trick Sidearms, it is probably the easiest to do. Keep this in mind with this throw. When you do it, remember to throw under the *opposite* leg. If you are a right-hander, throw under your left leg. If you are a left-hander, throw under your right leg.

Stand with your left side facing the target if you are throwing with the right hand. (The opposite throughout

A flying between-the-legs catch is beautiful to see when done with this great skill. (Ross R. Olney photo)

this and other throws if you are left-handed.) Raise your left leg and, using the standard Sidearm grip, bring the disc up and cock your wrist.

Swing your arm down, bringing your throwing hand under your thigh. The disc should be tilted at about a 45-degree angle with the top away from you. As the disc passes under your knee, snap your wrist and release.

You can do the same trick with your right leg raised even if you are a right-handed thrower (or your left leg if you are a left-handed thrower) but it is a little more difficult. Your hand and arm will tend to come into contact with your thigh sooner because you are raising the leg that is closer to the side where the throw is originating.

Another variation to this throw is the *Leaping Kick Sidearm.* Kick one leg high into the air and as it starts down, kick the other one up. At one brief point in time, both legs will be off the ground. Dancers call this a "hitchkick." That is the point at which you swing the disc down, uncock your wrist and release it. It will sail

72

away under *both* legs if you make your moves in coordination and release at the right instant.

Still another variation is the *Between-the-Legs Sidearm.* You will be using the same Sidearm grip but you will be facing the target squarely. Spread your feet wide apart and flex your knees, then cock your wrist and bring your arm behind you.

Push forward with your lower body and lift slightly to the ball of the foot on the side where you are throwing. With a quick unsnapping of the wrist, release forward between the legs.

To carry the Sidearm throw to its ultimate trickiness, there are also a couple of "blind" throws—that is, you throw without being able to see your target. One is done by bending forward and throwing the disc *back* between your legs; the other is done by throwing the disc around your waist to the rear. In both throws, you do not look where you are throwing (though you have certainly looked carefully before the throw to see where your target is). Use the standard Sidearm grip.

There are other trick throws that experts have developed and new ones are being invented all the time. Remember the Overhand Wrist Fling? You might want to throw the same type of throw, but under the leg instead of out to the right or left. Use the same grip (disc in the wedge of the hand, four fingers on top, and thumb underneath).

Or, upside down or right side up, invent some throws of your own. Upside down? Sure. For example, there is the *Upside Down Sidearm*. Grip the disc in the normal Sidearm grip (disc in the wedge, thumb on top, forefinger underneath, middle finger behind the rim in the cheek) but instead of throwing a normal Sidearm, bring the disc directly over the top of your head. Uncock your wrist and release the disc as you are shifting your weight forward and to the left. If the disc is released at about a 45-degree angle it will fly away upside down.

Try the *Upside Down Backhand*.

Use the Backhand grip with the thumb on top, the forefinger on the rim and the remaining fingers curled underneath, but throw the disc from a position behind the shoulder. The underside of the disc can be resting against your shoulder before the throw. The wrist should be well cocked. A right-hander should then step forward on the left foot, then the right foot, and release the disc at about a 45-degree angle upside down. Not easy, but you'll learn quickly with some practice. Be sure to release over the top and not sideways.

Why? Why not just use the Overhand Wrist Fling in the first place?

Just for fun, that's why.

That's what throwing the disc is all about.

How about one final trick throw that is said to have occurred to disc expert John Weyand in a dream? Naturally it is called the *Dream Shot* though it is actually an *Upside-Down Thumb Throw*. This is a throw that can fly out and down, skim inches off the ground, and then rise again. Or it can soar high and then rapidly sink.

Grip the disc in the usual Thumb Throw grip (thumb in the cheek and four fingers on top) and stand with your left side toward the target if you are a right-handed thrower. Hold the disc next to your bicep, coil your body to the right with both the wrist and the elbow cocked. Step forward on your left foot and bring the arm forward. Uncock your elbow, bringing the disc over the top of your head and at an upside-down angle. Snap the wrist forward and release. The disc will soar away upside down.

Practice will give you the control to make this a beautiful throw.

Remember this hint. Work on the basic throws throughout your practice on these advanced trick throws so that your groundwork of technique and style will not be affected. You can learn to make the disc curve where you want it to go by controlling the angle of release. You can learn to play the wind to make the disc do what you want it to do. By controlling the angle of the throw, you can cause the disc to hover and drop gently on the target and thus set up some of the catches described next (tipping, nail delays, etc.). You can practice skips, where the disc skims down, touches the surface, and rebounds, still under perfect control.

Do this first, though. Before you try skips, practice until your wrist is strong and the disc soars without a wobble. For the disc must touch the ground on the side and not with the leading edge for it to skip properly. You don't want it to lose any more of its spin than necessary, and you also don't want it to plow into the ground and stop.

Some modern experts are now working on a rolling throw that causes the disc to travel for a distance along the surface on its edge. A roller can be a great aid in a game of disc golf, where the disc must go around an obstacle or where it must remain very close to the ground because of overhanging bushes or branches.

Once you learn the ground skipping and rolling techniques, you might want to try air-bouncing. This is a very fancy throw where the disc actually bounces off a cushion of air and rises before it hits the ground. You can throw a bounce from a Backhand, but it takes practice and more practice. Throw down and forward but with the disc tilted slightly up at the leading edge.

Now let's try some trick catches.

The Tail Catch

This is a good one to start with. It is a simple catch once you have learned the basics; still, it looks fancy. Timing, however, is very important.

Allow the disc to pass over and behind you, then reach out and catch it (palm up or palm down, depending on how high it is) from *behind*.

Everybody will think you have missed it completely, but suddenly you *have* it!

The Tail Catch can be accomplished to the right, the

left, over your head, behind your back, or under or between your legs.

The Elbow Catch

Here's another fancy way to stop the disc under control. Stand with your arm bent and elbow out. Allow the disc to come in to your side, then clamp your arm down and trap it between your elbow and your side. With this catch as with the others, timing is important.

The Knee Catch

Done the same way as the Elbow Catch, only the disc is caught between the knees. Some experts manage a *Leaping Knee Catch*. They can perfectly judge the incoming disc and at the last possible instant leap into the air and trap the disc between their knees. Then they land without dropping it. A fancy catch to watch!

The Foot Catch

This can be accomplished with the same precise timing. Just drop to the ground on your back as the disc comes in, reach up with your feet and trap it between them.

Behind the Knees Catch

Give this fancy catch a try. Turn around as the disc approaches and allow it to strike you on the backs of your legs. Then, with perfect timing, drop to a squat and trap it between your lower leg and your upper leg. The catch is made if the disc doesn't hit the ground, so you can also give the next "hands-off" catch a try.

The Stomach Catch

Judge the incoming disc correctly and as it hits you in the midsection, bend over quickly and trap it. This one can also be done by leaping into the air and trapping the disc in your stomach (but you'll *really* have to practice to do this).

Flying disc competitions include a freestyle event where tricks (throws and catches) make winners. Most of the competitors have also learned flight-extending techniques that enhance the sport. One of the first things they learn is tipping.

Tipping

This is not a catch, but a way of setting up a catch— or even just extending a throw a little more. The disc is deflected by a finger, several fingers, a hand, a foot, a knee, an elbow, or even the top of the head. It is bumped back into flight while it is still spinning. It might be tipped (or tapped, as some disc flyers call it) into your own hand or into a partner's hand.

The basic tip is with one finger thrust lightly up underneath the disc as it is floating down to you. If the tip is done at the very center of the disc, it will pop back up. It will then settle again for an easy catch. The lighter the tip, the better the control. Don't slam a fist up into the disc. It will pop back up, but out of control and wobbling.

Tipping can be done with the disc right side up or upside down, spinning clockwise or counterclockwise, and with your right or left hand. There is a slight difference in where you touch the disc depending on which way it is spinning, but you will learn this quickly with experimentation.

Practice tipping techniques by spinning the disc up a few feet overhead. Hold it between your hands with your fingers spread on the rim, then spin it upward. It will float back down and you can tip.

Or double-tip, or triple-tip, or tip from finger to knee to hand, or some other combination. Tipping is fairly new in the sport of disc flying, but it is growing every day with zany experimental tips. One expert throws himself into a horizontal position in the air, tips with his foot, then rights himself and tips several times with other parts of his body before he finally catches the disc. This is something to see!

Tipping to a partner is great fun. Position yourself forward of your partner; then, when the disc comes in, tip it on its way. Try for accuracy, of course.

The Nail Delay

Here is yet another non-catch that enhances the game

TRICKY DISCS

for onlookers and offers you a chance for better disc

A perfect nail delay is shown by this disc expert.
(Ross R. Olney photo)

control. The idea is to get the disc to land on and continue spinning on your fingernail. The "delay" is because the final catch is held off during this maneuver.

Double your fist and extend your forefinger (or middle finger, if that feels more comfortable to you). Bend the finger at both joints so that it is flexible and so that only the nail and not the skin comes into contact with the underside of the disc.

Allow the disc to settle on your finger. Do not bring your finger up to the disc but, rather, *give* with the disc as it settles so that you do not disturb its attitude or its spin. Try to get as close to the center as possible.

It is very difficult to hit the exact center on the underside, especially where there is a tiny bulge of plastic. The spin of the disc will cause it to try to spin off and your fingernail will move toward the rim. Constant minor adjustments are necessary to hold a nail delay correctly.

Certain models of certain discs have an indentation in the center of the bottom, making nail delays much easier. Consider adding such a disc to your collection for just this purpose. You'll see the indented ones at the store. Or, if this type is not available, then look for one with a smooth bottom, with no bulge. Expert disc flyers can nail-delay a smooth-bottomed or indented disc until it stops spinning, but this takes practice. Experts also nail-delay for a time, then tip the disc on to a partner or into their other hand or for some other trick catch.

Here's a hint to help you with nail delays. Lubricate the disc (it won't affect the flight characteristics) with a silicone spray or a household wax at the center point of the bottom. Be careful, however, not to lubricate the rim area where you need to have a good, solid grip for throwing.

Two final tricks of the experts are *Airbrushing* and *Guiding*.

As the disc settles down toward you, cup your hand, aim into the wind, and gently strike the rim with your palm in the direction of spin. It is possible to use this Airbrushing technique more than once on the same flight, always moving the disc into the wind. As you move forward you can cause a series of floats with careful brushes of the disc. Practice until you get the feel of this exciting trick.

Guiding is simply deflecting the disc off one hand (or some other part of the body) and into the other hand for the catch.

It is possible, with long practice sessions, to learn to Airbrush and Guide with hands, feet, and other parts of the body and then use these tricks to finish with a trick Behind the Back or Between the Legs catch. There is no limit, and new tricks are being perfected every day in this young sport.

Most of them are truly poetic. They show athletic skill and smooth control of the disc—or they show very funny comedy which demonstrates still other techniques of disc control in ways that create audience enjoyment.

6
Canine
Catch-and-Fetch

It wasn't very long at all before somebody discovered that dogs love the flying disc. They seem to take to it naturally and accept it as an enjoyable part of their life. With a little pleasant work you can train your pet to catch a disc with hardly ever a miss.

That isn't all the fun, either. There are contests throughout the country leading to the champion dog disc-catcher. City, county, state and regional meets narrow the field, and in the fall each year the finalists compete at the Rose Bowl in California to determine the World's Champion K-9.

At formal contests, usually cosponsored by a pet food company, the local parks and recreation department, and the Wham-O Company, there is no restriction as to type and breed of dog (or type and breed of disc thrower, for that matter). Size or age of either is not important. They do prefer dogs who will behave around other dogs, but the important thing is how well the dog and master work together.

The most famous of all Catch and Fetch dogs is Ashley Whippet, shown here with his owner before a major contest. (Ross R. Olney photo)

The usual Catch-and-Fetch contest is done in time limit periods, with points awarded for successful catches at distances of at least fifteen yards. Extra points are given when the catch is made with all four paws off the ground.

The top dogs from each meet go on to the next meet, and competition gets more and more difficult. Finally there are nine regional champion dogs and their owners (or the person who has thrown for them through all levels of competition). Sponsors pay all travel, lodging, and food expenses for these teams to come to Pasadena for the finals. At one such final contest a dog by the name of Ashley Whippet leaped *nine feet into the air* to make a mighty catch. Ashley won, of course, to become World's Champion K-9.

Here are some of the contest rules at official Catch-and-Fetch contests.

1. There should be a timer, a scorekeeper, and an ob-

Ashley (in action) has been known to jump nine feet in the air *to catch a flying disc.* (Wayne Pinkstaff photo)

Everybody enjoys pitch and catch with a disc-catching dog. Here Bruce Jenner, Olympic decathlon champion, trains his dog Barney.
(Ross R. Olney photo)

server to make sure that all four paws are off the ground for extra points. No judging expertise is required, so just about anybody can do the job.

2. Any flying disc may be used for practice but it is preferred (though not required) that special Frisbee discs issued be used in actual competition. The discs are supplied free of charge to contestants.

3. Each dog will be given two minutes to catch as many throws as possible for points, with one point being awarded

A dog doesn't have to be large to be a catch-and-fetcher, as this little dog-gie shows. (Wayne Pinkstaff photo)

Now wait a minute! Yes, all paws off the ground means extra points, but not eight paws. (Ross R. Olney photo)

for every catch made and a bonus point awarded if the catch is made in mid-air, with all four paws off the ground.

4. All throws must be made from inside a circle or behind a line and for a distance of at least 15 yards. The thrower may step over the line to retrieve the disc, but must go back into the circle or behind the line to make the next throw.

5. One disc is to be used for the time period. If it becomes damaged, though, a new disc may be substituted.

6. Preliminary rounds may be held to cut down on a large field of dogs.

7. The person who throws for the dog in the preliminary competitions must continue to throw during the advanced contests. Helpers are not allowed on the field. Only in case of illness can this rule be modified and only one dog per entrant is allowed.

This beautiful shepherd (top left) *shows how he won the local contest to proceed on to the state finals.* (Ross R. Olney photo)

(Middle) *Even Ashley Whippet misses one occasionally.*
(Ross R. Olney photo)

(Bottom) *A great leap and a twisting, turning catch earns extra points for this dog.* (Ross R. Olney photo)

8. All dogs must be kept on a leash except during practice and competition.

9. Owners are responsible for clean-up for their own dogs.

10. It is advised that dogs be fed after the competition and not before.

11. Each owner must provide a container for water.

12. Dogs that cause undue distraction while other animals are performing may be penalized two points for each infraction.

13. Any dog which cannot be controlled by its owner and thus represents nuisance or hazard can be disqualified by officials.

14. Owners should keep their dogs out of the hot sun until their turn.

15. All dogs competing must have a valid license and proof of anti-rabies inoculation, where required by city or county ordinance.

Catch-and-Fetch contests are fun to watch and fun to be in, but you can also have fun with your dog in an informal way. You don't have to wait for a contest. In fact, training should be started months before if you expect your dog to become good at catching and fetching the flying disc.

Here are five tips:

1. Long-nosed dogs seem to do better than dogs with a snub nose. Snub-noses like bulldogs, pekingese and the like seem to lack mouth space and breath control for tough work like flying disc catching.

2. "Cheeky" dogs with jowels hanging down won't do as well, either. If you have a bassett hound, better train it for hunting.

3. Dogs dry out faster than people, so have plenty of water available during training sessions.

4. Dogs don't know when to quit. They'll play until they drop, especially a game they love like catching the flying disc. *You* watch, and give them a rest from time to time.

5. The whole trick is to be patient. Get your pet used to the disc without force or strain. You might even consider feeding or watering him from it. Teach him to jump for the disc while it is in your hand. Soon he will be jumping and catching when you toss it for a very short distance. Praise him lavishly every time he catches the disc. Before you know it, he'll be trying for it on longer and longer throws. Your pet wants to please you, and he enjoys catching the disc. But you must show him what you want him to do. All the while, teach him to bring the disc back to you. This will save time during contests when you are both working under the stopwatch.

7

Flying Disc Games

Years ago, when disc flying was an even younger sport than it is now, they molded an instruction into the underside of one popular model.

"Play catch, invent games," the words suggested.

Since then, though the words are no longer there, millions of disc flyers have taken the advice to heart. There are many, many games you can play with discs. Some of them are quite formal, with rules and regulation playing fields. Others are more informal. You just get together with a few players and go at it.

Other games are devised on the spot when disc throwers gather and use whatever space is available to get a contest going. The astronauts flew discs on the moon!

Disc flying has spread worldwide and into international competition. After all, it has three great advantages:

1. Flying the disc is low in cost.
2. Flying the disc offers a very low injury rate.
3. Flying the disc can be enjoyed many different ways.

TRICKY DISCS

Let's take a look at a few of the games disc flyers are playing today. Try them. Build on them. In strict and regulated competitions the rules are tight, but otherwise you can play as you wish. The most favorite game of all is listed first.

Throw and Catch

If you never play another flying disc game, you will catch on to the fun and excitement of the sport from this one. It is what it says it is. You throw the disc and you catch the disc. You can set your own limits on distance between players and on force and trickiness of throws and catches.

This is the game you see at picnics and on the beach and at the lakeside. This is the impromtu game, the game that begins when the disc comes out (somebody always seems to bring one along) and ends when the last player is called to dinner. You throw to him, he throws to her, she throws to somebody else and soon everybody is involved.

Who needs contests or competitions? *This* is the fun of flying the disc.

Very informal and a lot of fun is this game where the disc is rolled along the ground between a long row of legs. Watch the row weave back and forth like a snake as the disc rolls along (top right).

(Ross R. Olney photo)

(Middle) *Guts is a game of action and fury, where the thrower throws as hard and fast as he can.* (Ross R. Olney photo)

(Bottom) *The catchers try to catch the disc even though it has been thrown to be uncatchable, like this one skimming along the ground.*

(Ross R. Olney photo)

92

TRICKY DISCS

You can even play the game with yourself if a fair wind is blowing. Face into the wind and get ready for the *Boomerang Throw*. Use the standard Backhand grip and tilt the leading edge of the disc slightly upward as you throw. The disc will rise up into the wind, hover, and then as it drops it will come back to you. Experienced throwers can get the disc to come back to their hand with deadly accuracy. There is even an international event that involves this throwing trick (see Chapter Eight).

Throwing and catching can even work indoors if you have a large enough space or a small enough (or soft enough) disc. You can't throw a boomerang or get as fancy as you might wish, but you can have some fun.

Time in the Air

This is strictly an outdoor game. It is simple and direct and to the point. The idea is to see how long you can get a flying disc to fly. Time starts the instant the disc leaves your hand. Time stops the instant the disc hits the ground (or lands in a tree, or wherever). The winner is the one who manages the longest flight.

A tip: *use* the wind.

Sweet Georgia Brown

Does this name recall to you a famous basketball team? Of course. They are the Harlem Globetrotters. The

94

"Trotters" not only put on a great show, they are highly skilled basketball players as well.

Before each game they display their skill by forming a circle and passing the ball back and forth. Any pass is legal; any surprise move to take another player off guard is proper. Between-the-legs shots are common. Over the shoulder, from behind the back, bouncing off something or someone—anything goes.

The same is true with the flying disc game. Form a circle with as many players as you have and begin to throw the disc about. No order of throw, naturally. Just keep that disc moving, fast and furious, always trying to surprise one of the other players into dropping it.

Be prepared in this game, for the disc can move fast!

To add spice, you might declare before the game begins that anybody who drops the disc is out. The player left at the end is the winner.

A tip: make it clear ahead of time that the disc that is touched could have been caught. If it is beyond reach after an honest grab, it doesn't count as a drop.

Keep Away

This game is a variation of Sweet Georgia Brown. Players form a circle, then the one who has been chosen "it" gets in the center. The idea is to keep the disc in the ring but away from the one in the center. This means more accurate throws, for if the catcher drops the disc he must change places with the player in the center.

The other way for a player to get out of the center is to catch the disc. Then the thrower must go to the center and be "it." The one in the center is probably going to get hit by the disc, but the injury rate is very, very low.

Another tip: remember that you yourself may be in the center soon, so don't throw any blistering Backhands that might hurt.

Both Sweet Georgia Brown and Keep Away can be played indoors or outdoors.

Obstacle Course

This is a somewhat more complicated disc game, one that takes some setting up ahead of time. The game can be played indoors or outdoors (though with an inside game you should use a mini-disc rather than a regular size). Let's look at the outdoor version and you can modify trees to armchairs if it rains.

Obstacle Course, also called *Discothon* by some players, requires a disc for each player and a course that has been marked out ahead of time. Put each player's name on his or her disc with a felt-tip pen so that they will not be mixed up during the game. No player should throw any other player's disc.

Lay out a course of any length but be sure each player knows the course before the game starts. Use trees, poles, small buildings, bushes and other barricades as obstacles, marking each one with a ribbon. Sometimes a map is made of the course and a copy given to each player before the game.

The object is to get to the end of the course first (or, according to some rules, with the least number of throws). Players cannot carry their disc. It must be thrown from where it landed. Of course the obstacles will be in the way, so the disc must be thrown around them to follow the course.

In this game, rules do not permit detours or shortcuts, or getting in the way of another player's throw.

Here's a hint for accurate throwing, in this game or any other. If your disc is turning over too often, you are using too much arm and too little wrist action. The faster it moves and the slower it spins, the more likely it will be to turn over and drift off target.

It might be helpful to have one or more judges following the action here and in certain other outdoor games. Players might get spread out and it could help to have some impartial observers watching everybody. There must be a judge at the finish line to see who gets there first and to report the number of throws (if you are using that method of judging).

If the disc lands off the course, the player must throw it from where it landed to get it back on the course. Remember that you can run as fast as you like after a throw, but hurrying too much might hurt your game. Take your time (always within reason, that is) and go for accuracy of throw rather than speed of foot. That's how the winners do it.

Ringer

This game can only be played with the Whiz Ring type of disc, the type that has an open center. Indoors, it should be played with a Mini Whiz Ring. Outdoors, with the larger competition models. The game is played like horseshoe pitching, with a stake (or two stakes set at a distance apart) as a target. Outdoors, you can also use any convenient tree limb stub, fencepost, or other stake the ring will fit over.

Score five points for a "ringer" and fewer points, depending on how close you land to the target, for a miss. In this game it is permissible to knock your opponent's disc away from the target with a good throw of your own. But your opponent can also knock your disc away. Count the score after each "set" of discs has been thrown. The number in the set can depend on how many discs you have available to throw, but should be the same for each player.

Accuracy Toss

Any type of disc, any size, will work. You'll need a series of "bull's-eye" rings for a target, or any available straight line. If you are using a line, the game is much like the old-fashioned penny toss game (and is sometimes called "lag" by disc players).

The idea is to get your disc or set of discs closest to the target. If you are outdoors, the target will be farther away (and you will probably want to use full-sized discs). An outdoor bull's-eye or line can be made with chalk, ribbon, or even lines of stones.

If you have a bull's-eye, you can assign a certain number of points for each ring. When the disc falls entirely

This ring is for accuracy throws, but it can also serve as a hole for disc golf. Looks like a dead center hit on this throw.

You don't need store-bought "holes" for Frisbee golf. Nature provided this hole, and course organizers marked it. Just pass the disc between the trees, as the arrows indicate.

within that ring, that number of points is awarded. If the disc falls on a line, the smaller number of points is awarded. As a general rule, the center ring will be worth ten points, the next one eight, and so on according to the number of rings you have.

There is a difference if you are throwing to a line instead of a bull's eye target. Since this is an accuracy event, there should be a point at the center of a twenty-foot-long line that is worth the most. Scoring a line-throw game, then, is like this:

The center spot on the line is worth 25 points. Off the line, but within five feet on either side, is worth 10 points. On the line but not on the center spot is worth 25 points *minus* the number of feet your disc has landed from the center spot. If you are on the line but five feet away from the center spot, deduct five points and take twenty points as your score.

You and your competitors can throw as many discs as you have available (the same number for each player) before scoring, and discs can be knocked away from the line before scoring by an accurate throw from an opponent.

100

Marathon

This is an exciting flying disc game that can easily be organized between groups throwing at a picnic or beach. Get several pairs of players together, each with a disc of their choice (probably the disc they have been throwing).

Have them stand in two rows along parallel lines marked on the ground or already there as street edges, pathways, field markings, etc. The lines should be no more than 15 or 20 yards apart. Partners should stand facing each other across the space between the lines. Allow about 5 yards between teams so that each player has some room to move.

To begin the game, ask a bystander to start counting loudly, with a number every ten seconds.

"One!" the counter will shout then, ten seconds later, "two! . . . three! . . ." and so on, every ten seconds. At each number, the disc is thrown from one partner to the other. It should be thrown as accurately as possible, as gently as possible, making it as easy as possible to catch. For if the disc is dropped, or if the catcher must step over the line to catch it, that team is "out." The count keeps going until only one team is left. They are the winners.

Speedthrow

If you want to improve your timing, this is the game for you. But you are going to take a chance on broken fingernails or maybe even a jammed finger. This is definitely an outdoor game.

Stand facing your partner while any other teams in the game gather to watch the fun. You should be about 15 or 20 yards apart. You'll need a judge or a bystander to time this event.

Begin throwing the disc back and forth as fast as you can, counting each throw aloud. The idea is to throw it thirty times (counting "one . . . two . . . three . . . four . . ." with each throw) without dropping it and remaining on the lines or behind them (though this wastes time, since you must come back to the line for each throw). If you drop the disc or step over the line or throw from behind the line, your team is finished.

The team that can accomplish this rather difficult task (thirty clean throws and catches as fast as possible) in the best time is the winner.

Disc Golf

Today there are a number of disc golf courses set up around the country, and new ones are being designed and constructed all the time. The game is the invention of Spud Melin of Wham-O and golfers ("real" golfers) are still shaking their heads. The first permanent course was built in Thousand Oaks, California, by disc expert George Sappenfield.

Unlike regular golf, disc golf can be played at almost any park or recreation area with little advance set-up.

You can use birdbaths, doorways, football goalposts, flag-poles, the "V" between two tree limbs, garbage cans, or road signs as your targets. Park benches work. Any of these, and any other natural or available object, can work as the "holes" for your course. You will find that every

Disc golf can be played with very informal objects as "holes," or you can now get real, official disc golf holes like this one (insert).
(Ross R. Olney photo)

Disc expert Mike Conger demonstrates how to hit a hole in disc golf.
(Ross R. Olney photo)

103

one of your disc-throwing skills will be called upon to make a round.

After a few rounds of your course you can even assign a par to each "hole" and then practice to make par. There is no reason why you cannot have a stand of trees blocking a hole—an accurate roll throw will get the disc through. Regular disc golf courses have doglegs, uphill and downhill fairways, and water traps. Each hole on a regular course that has been built for disc golf has some type of opening or ring through which the disc must pass. Otherwise, the rules of golf can be followed very closely.

Lowest score wins, with each throw being one point.

There are two rather complex team games with the disc that require skill and stamina and a great deal of practice. These two games began as impromptu beach and picnic games but now many colleges have teams and national playoffs are held. The competition is rugged, and fans cheer with as much enthusiasm as for their college football or basketball team.

Fields are marked for both these games. Players must train, as competition for a spot on the team is keen. The difference is that a disc is used instead of a ball, and finesse rather than brute force. Both games are exciting to watch.

Ultimate

Ideally, this complex team game is played on a 60-yard

by 40-yard field, with a 30-yard end zone at each end of the field. There are seven players—very skilled at both throwing and catching—on each team. The idea of this intercollegiate and interscholastic and club game is to score by passing to a teammate in the opponent's end zone. Players may run except when they are holding the disc in this fast-moving, non-contact game that requires teamwork and passing magic.

Of course the other team is guarding and blocking and trying to prevent a score and to get the disc for themselves.

Ultimate is a very exciting game for players. There are always dramatic throws under extreme pressure and some catches that must be seen to be believed.

Guts

This is the other major disc team game. They probably named it this because you need courage (guts) to play it. If you are ever going to get sliced with a fast-moving disc, it will happen during a Guts game.

The rules are simple. Two teams of five players each square off against each other 14 meters (about 15 yards) apart. They throw as hard and as fast as they can. The idea is to throw with such force, deception, or skill that you cause the other team to miss the catch. If you do, and the disc was within reach, you get a point.

If they catch it, you get no point. To make things a little tougher, if your throw is bad (outside a certain distance) *they* get the point. Naturally, when they catch

A miss! The disc has bounced off the center player and away through the air. (Ross R. Olney photo)

the disc (no point) they get to throw it back to your side. Now *they* want *you* to miss it.

You can see that the game of Guts is fast, furious, and exciting. If you get a chance to see one, don't miss it.

106

8

The IFA, Ratings and Tournaments

The throwing of the flying disc had become quite popular by the early 1960s. Anywhere, anytime, you might come across a formal game and you were always stumbling over individual disc players. But there was no communication between areas. There was no formal arrangement for competitions, no clearinghouse for information on disc flying.

One was needed, for disc flying was obviously here to stay.

Ed Headrick, who was general manager of Wham-O and who first saw the flying disc as a sport rather than a toy, created the International Frisbee Association (now the International Frisbee disc Association). Almost immediately he was swamped with requests for information and membership applications. An informational newsletter called the *IFA Newsletter* proved valuable to members.

Today the IFA has more than 85,000 members around the world. They range from expert competition players

Before the crowd arrives (more than 55,000 in 1978) the disc experts from around the world begin to practice at the Rose Bowl.

(Ross R. Olney photo)

to men and women and boys and girls who toss discs for fun and relaxation. The organization blossomed even more under the guidance of its current leader, Dan "Stork" Roddick. Stork, an expert player, started his own publication in 1974. It was called *Flying Disc World*. It was an instant success, as the *IFA Newsletter* had been.

In 1975 the IFA was restructured to take into consideration its own rapidly expanding membership. A number of regional competitions were established to help players qualify for the popular World Frisbee Championships at the Rose Bowl each year.

A new director had been hired. The *IFA Newsletter* was combined with Roddick's *Flying Disc World*, the new publication was named *Frisbee World*, and Roddick took over as Director of the IFA and editor of the publication. Women's champion Jo Cahow is Roddick's chief assistant and feature editor of the magazine.

What can the IFA do for you? Whether you are a

108

casual saucer tosser or a real "Frisbee disc freak," you might enjoy membership. The IFA has set up "standards of proficiency" to provide every member with a way to judge his or her increasing skill with the disc. These standards are accepted throughout the world and identifying patches are proudly worn by members.

The IFA is also dedicated to giving recognition to accomplishments in disc flying, to improving disc flying techniques, and to increasing total proficiency in the use of the flying disc.

Who needs "standards of proficiency"? What if you just happen to enjoy flipping a disc about, and have no thought of ever competing or practicing the necessary hours to polish a special throw or catch? Then you fit in with most of the members of the organization. The first, and most popular, division of membership in the IFA is the Novice.

Woman champion Jo Cahow, an official in the International Frisbee disc Association, watches a competition with a friend. (Ross R. Olney photo)

109

Contestants warm up for an event at a contest.   (Ross R. Olney photo)

As a Novice, you hold a lifetime membership card, you display a certificate on your wall, and you receive a copy of the Official Proficiency Manual (in case you ever decide to advance).

The next step up the proficiency ladder in the IFA is the Expert classification. An Expert is a member who has passed the Expert Proficiency Test. The passing of this test and others can be certified by two other members in good standing or, if they are not available, then three members of the community involved in organized sports in the parks or schools (a local park director, for example, would fit on this panel, as would any high school coach or athletic director).

An Expert must prove his or her skill by making the following throws and catches:

1. Four straight flights
2. Two right curve flights

110

3. Two left curve flights

4. Two hovering, or floating, flights

5. Two skip flights

6. Four distance throws (two upwind, two down-wind), all of at least 30 yards distance.

7. Four sidearm or underhand flights

8. Two consecutive catches with the right hand

9. Two consecutive catches with the left hand

10. Two consecutive catches behind the back

11. Two consecutive catches between the legs

If you can manage these throws and catches, you qualify as an Expert according to the IFA. If you can show these skills to two other members in good standing, you will receive a new wall certificate and ID card (upon receipt of a $5 fee to cover IFA costs).

Want to go on into the ranks of the competitors? The next ranking is the Master division. Here it begins to get a little tougher.

A Master must exhibit the following skills to three member-examiners:

1. Four straight flights

2. Four right curve flights

3. Four left curve flights

4. Four hover flights

5. Four skip flights

6. Distance flights with a 40-yard minimum average, upwind and downwind.

7. Two consecutive self-caught flights

8. Two overhand wrist flip flights

9. Two alternate style flights with a grip not used before.

10. Four consecutive right hand catches

11. Four consecutive left hand catches

12. Three consecutive behind-the-back catches

13. Three consecutive between-the-legs catches

14. Three consecutive behind-the-head catches

15. Three consecutive finger catches

16. Three consecutive tip catches

A Master receives a new black metal embossed wallet card, a new wall certificate, and fifteen discs from the Wham-O company for instruction (for a $7.50 handling fee).

There is one final classification. There is a World Class Master division of the IFA for the top throwers and catchers in the world. These tests are given only at regional IFA offices and are set up by appointment. But if you can pass the World Class Master tests, you are among the best disc fliers of all. Here is a brief outline of what you must be prepared to do. You can get more information from the IFA on all of these tests, and on membership.

All of these throwing tests must be made from within a 4-yard circle and to a catcher who may not step out of another 4-yard circle 30 yards away. You must be accurate as well as highly skilled.

1. Nine straight flights using three different styles

2. Nine hover flights using three different styles

3. Nine right curve flights using three different styles

4. Nine left curve flights using three different styles

5. Nine skip flights using three different styles

6. Three consecutive multiple skips

7. Three consecutive straight rollers

8. Three consecutive curve rollers

9. Four consecutive flights (2 upwind, 2 downwind) with an average distance of at least 60 yards

10. Two consecutive 8-second, self-caught flights or two consecutive 120-foot self-caught flights

11. Three consecutive behind-the-back catches

12. Three consecutive between-the-legs catches

13. Three consecutive behind-the-head catches

14. Two of the following combination catches:

a. Any combination using a kick tip followed by a trick catch

b. Any tipping combination using three different body parts followed by a trick catch

c. A kick-up of a roller followed by a trick catch

d. Any combination using at least three Airbrushes followed by a trick catch, but not a one-finger catch

e. Any combination using at least a two-second nail delay followed by a trick catch, but not a one-finger catch

If you can accomplish this difficult string of throws and catches, and do it before a panel of other experts who are judging you, you qualify as a World Class Master.

Upon payment of a $10 fee to the IFA for handling and record-keeping, you will be issued a gold metal wallet card, a wall certificate, 25 flying discs from Wham-O, and a World Class Master sew-on patch for your jacket or warm-up suit. You are also eligible to purchase a gold

TRICKY DISCS

World Class Master warm-up suit with your name on the jacket.

Wearing such a suit at any contest identifies you as one of the best in the world of flying discs.

If you want to join the International Frisbee disc Association as a Novice, send your membership fee ($4) with your name and address to IFA, Box 970, San Gabriel, CA 91776.

Can you guess how many real experts there are in the organization? According to the most recent count, there are about 400 Masters and fewer than 100 World Class Masters.

Club Formation

One of the most important elements in the IFA is the vast group of local disc clubs. It is from these groups that

This competitor makes a flying catch under her leg during a freestyle event.
(Wayne Pinkstaff photo)

the disc players come; it is as local club members that they get their first experience as competition players. The clubs, affiliated under the IFA, serve as a means of communication between players from different areas. They help in the training of players who one day might want to compete in the national tournaments.

Any group of fifteen or more players anywhere in the country usually qualifies for membership. Such a group may apply for affiliate status with the IFA. The only requirement is that 75 percent of the group be registered as members of the IFA, or that such a number then registers.

"We believe," says Stork Roddick, "that you will find membership in the IFA an important part of your Frisbee disc experience, no matter what your level of skill or favorite form of play. We look forward to your membership."

He means it. The IFA will help your group in any way they can to get started as an affiliate group, and will give you all the information you need to hold local contests.

Competitions

There are many local and state championships held every year, sponsored by local clubs. The clubs might be working with other local merchants or businesses as co-sponsors to help provide prizes. These local contests are often the first taste of competition for new disc players. From there they can go on to the larger contests.

No contest would be complete without a violent and fast game of Guts.
(Wayne Pinkstaff photo)

National Championship Series meets are held throughout the country. There are fifteen of them, generally hosted by the local IFA club in that area. Through these meets, disc players qualify for the World Frisbee Championships held each year in California.

Team Championships are held each year to decide an Eastern Champion and a Western Champion in Ultimate. National Championship games are also held in Guts.

Open to all boys and girls fifteen years old and younger are the World Junior Frisbee disc Championships. These meets are held throughout the United States and are usually cosponsored by Wham-O and the local parks and recreation department. They run from about June of each year through August until all the regional finals are completed, then National Finals are held the latter part of each year.

The World Frisbee Championship, held in August, is a contest for the cream of the crop, the best disc throwers and catchers in the world. World titles are awarded in several categories including Freestyle, Distance, Frisbee Golf, and Maximum Time Aloft. There are three divisions in this competition: Men, Women, and Seniors (forty-five years old and older).

You will see disc flying that is difficult to believe at a World Frisbee Championship. Players do next to impossible things with the disc, tricks well beyond the requirements for World Class Master. The discs seem alive in the hands of these super-experts, responding to their wishes almost as if guided by the invisible wire "invented" by Fred Morrison so many years ago.

Disc Records

Can you guess what some of the current records are? They will amaze you.

Take distance, for example. The current records for distance, measured on a straight line from where the disc is thrown to where it first lands, is calculated for both indoor and outdoor throws.

Indoors: Men, 284 feet; women, 222.5 feet; seniors, 174 feet.

Outdoors: Men, 412 feet; women 283.5 feet; seniors, 230 feet.

The disc is a blur at the right in this photo as a distance competitor lets it fly with all his might. Hundred-yard throws are now common in distance competitions. (Ross R. Olney photo)

Time for some fun. Contestants at the world championship games line up for the photographer in a unique way. Then somebody tries to hit him with a disc. (Ross R. Olney photo)

These are *long* disc throws. They take strength, co-ordination, and a real knowledge of disc flight characteristics.

Records are also kept in the "T.R.&.C." category. This means throw, run, and catch. These boomerang throws are a sight to see as the player hurls the disc with all the strength and skill he or she can muster, all the time with the knowledge that it won't count if it can't be caught by the same player. Here are the current records in this zany event:

Men, 247.5 feet; women, 152.5 feet; seniors, 116 feet.

That takes skillful throwing and catching!

Accuracy is measured according to strict rules that require many direct hits during a contest of 28 throws.

Here are the direct hits through a 67.5-inch hoop target 35 feet away: Men, 21 of 28; women, 15 of 28; seniors, 15 of 28.

Maximum Time Aloft is another area where records are kept. The world MTA record for men is an astounding 15 seconds. For women it is 9.9 seconds and for seniors, 9.5 seconds. If that doesn't sound like a lot of time, try to keep a disc in the air for more than 3 or 4 seconds. You'll soon see that these are amazing records.

There are also world records for Freestyle and Frisbee Golf, but these depend, of course, on the individual player's performance at the time. They are judged on a level of difficulty of throws and catches and, in Freestyle, the creativity and consistency of the player's efforts. Freestyle is one of the real crowd-pleasers at any competition.

9

Care and Maintenance

Not many of us worry like the champions. They use a disc only a few times, then they get out a new one. Even the plastic threads that begin to show around the edges after a few hard landings can affect their throws. So they need a perfectly formed, threadless disc, often with each new contest throw.

You and I don't. We can use a disc over and over until it is squashed by a truck or lands in a place where a new one is cheaper than the risk of retrieving the old one. But even the novice disc thrower wants his or her disc to be in as perfect condition as possible.

So, when the disc gets rough on the edges, get out the steel wool and polish it. Smooth it off so that jagged edges won't affect the speed, direction, and accuracy of your throw.

Cleaning the Disc

There are experts like Dr. Stancil Johnson, mentioned earlier as the author of a fine book on flying discs, who

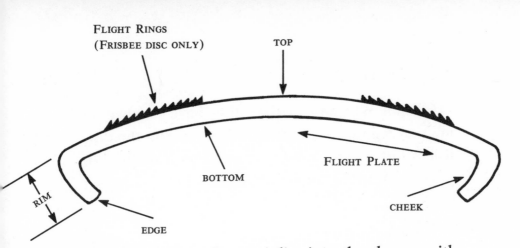

FLIGHT RINGS
(FRISBEE DISC ONLY)

TOP

FLIGHT PLATE

BOTTOM

CHEEK

RIM

EDGE

recommend that you take your disc into the shower with you. The truth is, soap and water are the best way to clean any plastic disc. Alcohols and other solvents can melt the surface, so stay with warm water (as warm as you can stand and still feel comfortable) and a mild soap. Don't let the water get too hot for your hands, for that is also too hot for your flying disc.

Sunlight

Sunshine is fine during play, but be sure you don't put away your disc in direct sunlight. Don't toss it in the back of the car or on a shelf near a window where it can bake in the sun. Sun will bleach the color and can also make your disc brittle.

Identification

To be sure your discs stay with you and don't become somebody else's property, mark each one on the bottom with a felt-tip pen. Your name and address should do it; then if the disc does become lost you might eventually get it back.

121

TRICKY DISCS

Certain Wham-O Frisbee discs have numbers molded in. You register the number when you buy the disc; then if it is lost it can be dropped into any mailbox. Wham-O pays the postage for its return to you.

Rough Surfaces

Even amateur players usually reserve their betters discs for playing on softer surfaces. Skip shots off concrete will quickly damage the edges of any disc, leaving what experienced players call "disc hair." This is the fuzzy, stringy, soft edge developed by a hard, spinning collision.

Some of it can be removed with steel wool, but generally the disc has been terminally injured after a few days of such shots. Polish the edges and use the disc for practice or canine catch-and-fetch sessions, but don't count on it when accurate throws are needed. The aerodynamics have probably changed due to the change along the edges.

Cracked or Torn Discs

This is a serious problem that often calls for permanent retirement. Glue and tape might help for a while, but sooner or later the disc must be retired to your non-working collection. Meanwhile, think of what that glue or tape is doing to the flight characteristics.

A few disc players have perfected a technique of using "donor" discs to repair a more favored disc. They do this by melting the edges of the crack together with a soldering iron, then dripping melted plastic from the donor disc into the crack in the disc they are trying to preserve. They use a butane torch for the melting. The resulting patch is scraped with a sharp knife or razor to blend it in as smoothly as possible. Finally, the joint can be sandpapered.

Stancil Johnson says that champion disc player Vic Malafronte has a disc he repaired in seven different places before the first tear finally reopened. Malafronte also has a "Frankenstein" disc made of parts from seven other discs.

So if you have a favorite disc that has been seriously injured, you can try this technique before retiring it permanently. The experts suggest using Wham-O's Moonlighter Frisbee disc as the donor, because the plastic from this disc is of the very highest grade and tends to flow the most smoothly.

Disc Transport

You can buy all sorts of disc accessories if you really want them. Available to disc players through local sporting goods stores, toy stores, and by mail order are a wide variety of T-shirts and shorts to wear while disc throwing; identification name buttons for contests; special transfers to personalize your discs; books, patches, and even bumper stickers.

There is one other item that every disc fan should consider buying. It is a disc bag for carrying your flyers to and from the playing field. These bags are specially made of tight-weave canvas. They have a shoulder strap, side pockets for discs, and a center pouch for other supplies and for your wallet, keys, loose change, etc. Most of them have a "D" ring on the outside so that you can loop a towel through and keep it readily available to wipe your hands during a game or contest.

A disc bag protects your discs, keeping them from rolling around on the floor of the car and getting scratched and torn. It is a good investment for every player.

Tricky discs are only "tricky" in the variety of things they can be made to do and in the many ways you can have fun with them. Otherwise they are easy to master and can become a lifetime pleasure.

You've probably already started, but if not, give one a try. You'll never regret it.

For Further Information

Magazine

Frisbee World
c/o International Frisbee
disc Association
P.O. Box 970
San Gabriel, CA 91776
($5 per year, 6 issues)

Disc Collector Exchange and Purchase

The Frisbee Clearing House
225 Circle Drive
Las Vegas, Nev. 89101

The Factory Connection
c/o International Frisbee
disc Association
P.O. Box 970
San Gabriel, CA 91776

Flying Disc Books

Frisbee Fun by Margaret
R. Poynter
Julian Messner, Inc.
1230 Avenue of the
Americas
New York, N.Y. 10020

Frisbee by the Masters by
Charles Tips
Celestial Arts Publishing
Company
231 Adrian Road
Millbrae, CA 94030

Frisbee by Dr. Stancil
E. D. Johnson
Workman Publishing
Company, Inc.
231 E. 51st St.
New York, N.Y. 10022

125

TRICKY DISCS

Frisbee, A Player's Handbook by Dan Poynter & Mark Danna
Parachuting Publications
P.O. Box 4232-R
Santa Barbara, CA 93103

Disc Demonstration Teams

Victor Malafronte
Propell Enterprises, Inc.
2450 El Camino Real, Suite 108
Palo Alto, CA 94306

Frisbee South
Tom Monroe
617 Cleermont
Huntsville, Ala. 35801

Air Aces Three
Professional Frisbee Team
P.O. Box 7866
Ann Arbor, Mich. 48107

The Aces
Professional Frisbee Team
655 Harmony Lane
Glenview, Ill. 60025

Wind Song
4237 B Monroe Drive
Boulder, Colo. 80303

New England Frisbee Athletics
Professional Frisbee Team
Box 333
Amherst, Mass. 01002

Frisbee Camp

Craigmeur
Green Pond Road
Newfoundland, N.J. 07435

Disc Training Films

Jammersports Films
P.O. Box 4331
Boulder, Colo. 80306

Canine Flying Disc Information

Canine Frisbee
Contest Headquarters
5430 Van Nuys Blvd.
Van Nuys, CA 91401

Index

airbrushing, 20, 82
All American model, 27
angle of release, 34
Ashley Whippet, 84–85, 88
Barclay, Richard, 16–17
baseball, 10
basketball, 10
Bridgeport, Conn., 15
Bunyan, Paul, 15, 28
Cahow, Jo, 108–109
Canine Catch and Fetch, 14, 83ff.
catches, *see* disc catches
Cinemataggio, Antonio "Lens," 15, 17
Cole, Elbert "Mole," 16
Conger, Mike, 103
Danna, Mark, 2
Delta Upsilon, 16, 17
disc catches
  behind the back, 59–61
  behind the head, 62–64
  behind the knees, 77–78
  between the legs, 61–62
  delayed, 61
  elbow, 77
  finger, 64–65
  foot, 77
  knee, 77
  leaping, 77
  sandwich, 58–59
  stomach, 78
  tail, 76–77
disc flight characteristics
  airfoil, 28
  attitude, 31
  force, 33
  forward motion, 28–29
  lift, 28–29
  pitch, 31–32
  roll, 32

  spin, 28, 33
disc games
  accuracy toss, 27, 98–99
  discothon, 96
  golf, 10, 100, 102–104
  guts, 22, 37, 46–47, 92, 105–106, 116
  keep away, 95–96
  marathon, 12, 101
  obstacle course, 96–98
  ringer, 27, 98
  speedthrow, 101–102
  Sweet Georgia Brown, 94–95
  time in the air, 94
  throw and catch, 92
  ultimate, 23, 104–105
disc hair, 122
disc records, 117
disc throws
  backhand, 33, 37–42
  behind-the-back backhand, 68–70
  behind-the-back sidearm, 70–71
  between-the-legs sidearm, 73
  boomerang, 94
  dream shot, 74–75
  finger flip, 66–68
  hooked thumb, 51–52
  leaping kick sidearm, 72–73
  overhand wrist fling, 34, 48–50, 73–74
  sidearm, 34, 42–44
  thumber, 34, 46–48
  under-the-leg sidearm, 71–72
  underhand, 33, 45
  upside-down backhand, 74
  upside-down thumb throw, 74–75
disc types
  All American, 27

TRICKY DISCS